## About the Author

Michael A Potter is an International Management Development Trainer, Writer, Speaker, Globalist, People Expert and HR Consultant. He has been CEO of MPA Consulting Ltd, Manchester, UK, for the last 20 years.

Michael is one of the UK's leading training and management development consultants and has worked in an advisory capacity for a variety of top businesses including, Rolls Royce, HSBC, the BBC, Cyprus Popular Bank, Financial Services Authority UK, Philippine Airlines, Citibank, British Energy British Nuclear Fuels Limited and the National Health Service UK.

Michael holds an MBA and a 1st degree in Business Studies from the University of Liverpool UK together with an MA in Organisational Analysis and Behaviour from University of Lancaster UK. He is also a Chartered Fellow of the UK's Chartered Institute of Personnel and Development. He is an active member of the North European HRM Forum, and a former visiting lecturer to the University of Liverpool.

Throughout his career, Michael has presented at conferences, delivered training workshops and seminars in numerous countries across Europe, Middle East, Africa and Asia. In 2012 he launched his new People Management Model titled *"The New People Matrix Management Model"* which has since been successfully presented in various countries across the world.

Michael also offers a one-day practice workshop to support this publication further. He can be reached at 0161 776 4383. His email address is: mike.potter@mpa-consultants.co.uk.

All rights reserved. No part of this publication may be reproduced, stored in a retrieval system, or transmitted in any form or by any means, electronic mechanical, photocopying, recording, or otherwise without the prior permission of the publishers.

First Published 2008

Second Edition 2015 published as *Mentoring In the Fast Lane*

This book is sold subject to the condition that it shall not, by way of trade or otherwise be lent, resold, hired out, or otherwise circulated without the publisher's prior consent in any form of binding or cover other than that in which it is published and without a similar condition including this condition being imposed upon the subsequent purchaser.

© Michael A Potter, 2008, 2015

ISBN: 978-1-4475-6579-6

**British Library Cataloguing-in-Publication Data**

A CIP record for this book is available from the British Library.

Printed and bound in Great Britain by LuLu: London

http://www.lulu.com

http://www.map-int.com

# Contents

| | | |
|---|---|---|
| Introduction | | 6 |
| **Part 1** | **CLARIFICATION of MENTORING** | 7 |
| 1. | **Derivation of the word 'Mentor'** | |
| | Definitions | |
| | What mentoring is not? | 9 |
| 2. | **Change** | 10 |
| | Areas of change | |
| 3. | **Mentoring Process** | 13 |
| | Why mentoring? | 14 |
| | Characteristics of mentoring | 15 |
| 4. | **Mentor characteristics** | 17 |
| | Positive | |
| | Negative | |
| | Notes on 'Wise Counsellor' | 18 |
| | Key points | 20 |
| 5. | **Roles** | 21 |
| | Organisation | 22 |
| | Organiser/Administrator | 23 |
| | Line Manager/Supervisor | 24 |
| | Mentor | 26 |
| | Trainee/Learner | 28 |
| 6. | **Pitfalls** | 30 |

http://www.map-int.com

| 7. | Learning Styles Questionnaire | 31 |
|---|---|---|
| | Scoring | 36 |
| | Learning Styles Analysis | 37 |

**Part 2**  **EXPLORATION of MENTORING**  **45**

1. **Learning Cycle and Styles**  45

2. **Kolb's Learning Cycle**  46
   Using Kolb's Learning Cycle  48
   Learning styles – summary  50
   Using learning styles and cycle  52

3. **Skills for Mentoring**  53
   Giving Attention  53
   Interpersonal skills  54
   Listening  57
   Questioning  59
   Objective-setting  63
   Facilitating  65
   Networking  66
   Feedback  67
   Coaching  68
   Counselling  71

| Part 3 | **IMPLEMENTING** | **75** |
|---|---|---|
| 1. | **Preparation** | **75** |
| 2. | **Induction** | **77** |
| 3. | **The First Meeting** | **81** |
|  | Manager of the Relationship | 83 |
|  | Interpreter of the Programme | 86 |
|  | Assessor to monitor progress | 88 |
|  | Coach | 89 |
|  | Counsellor | 91 |
| 4. | **A successful counselling session** | **93** |
| 5. | **Mentor characteristics checklist** | **97** |
| 6. | **Benefits of Mentoring** | **99** |

Reading List     101

# Introduction

## 1. AIM

This book will provide a practical introduction to the mentoring concept and its implementation for graduate trainees.

## 2. Objectives

- A. **CLARIFICATION** of the mentor concept and the place of mentoring today. Development of roles associated with mentoring.

- B. **EXPLORATION** of ideas and tools to aid good mentoring practice.

- C. **IMPLEMENTATION** of mentoring for graduate trainees.

- D. **GRADUATE PROGRAMME** requirements, roles and responsibilities.

# Part 1

# CLARIFICATION of MENTORING

## 1. Derivation of the word 'Mentor'

'Mentor' derived from Greek *mene* – meaning think (*mens* in Latin for mind).

In Greek mythology, Odysseus (Ulysses in Latin), an Ithacan king, left his friend Mentor, an Ithican noble, as a wise counsellor to the prince Telemachus who would reign.

This mythology Mentor was also a disguise for Athene, a goddess, hence access to wisdom.

## Definitions

### 'Mentoring'

'A protected confidential relationship and a set of processes where an experienced person offers help and support to facilitate the leaning and development of another less experienced.'

'A means of accelerating learning and change'

'Off-line help by one person to another in making significant transitions in knowledge, work or thinking.'

http://www.map-int.com

## 'Mentor'

'An experienced and trusted counsellor.'

'Wise counsellor'

## 'Trainee, Protégé, Mentee or Learner'

*(Mentee not yet in dictionary)*

'Learner is preferred as it focuses on the real purpose of mentoring'

'Learning is a relatively permanent change in behaviour resulting from practice and repetition.'

**THE BUSINESS OF MENTORING IS LEARNING.**

http://www.map-int.com

## What mentoring is not?

**It is NOT:**

- A replacement for conventional training.

- Intended to undermine the supervisor/subordinate couplet.

- An easy option.

- Tutor as in tutor/student.

- Instructor as in instructor/trainee.

- Manager as in manager/subordinate.

- Friend as in friend at court.

- Protégé as in favourite.

## 2.
# Change

Change today is rapid, radical, discontinuous and all embracing, affecting the individual and society in ways giving little time for adaptation. It is technology driven and demands coping strategies that are increasingly the responsibility of individuals themselves.

Radical change of complex systems intrinsically introduces extensive unpredictability. With no guarantees, the best response is the capacity to learn-to-learn allowing a chameleon-like reaction to most circumstances. This, however, is not a typical product of our education system and the new graduate needs to rapidly assimilate new ideas, attitudes and demands.

Mentoring, applicable across a wide range of circumstances and accommodating of any other initiatives, has proved an extremely successful strategy.

# Areas of change

### Society

Consumerism and individualism with fragmentation of community controls, rights emphasised over responsibility and status collapse of past social anchors have introduced social mobility, voluntary and compulsory, that means people find stable situations hard to find. Farming, manual, craft and clerical jobs are all in decline or shipped overseas, whilst professional and technical jobs have the largest projected expansion even over management, services and others.

**Market**

Since consumers have become progressively 'greyer, greener and wiser', markets have moved up into more sophisticated, quality, added-value products and services with fierce competition and requiring a skill-force rather than a workforce. Markets are now global.

**Organisations...**

...need cultural change, often almost continually. They are frequently radical and dramatic, flatter and leaner, merging into new structures that are fluid and adaptable are only the start, with command and control management on the wane and semi-autonomous work teams, multi-disciplinary and temporary in nature, becoming commonplace. Organisations de-layer and eliminate jobs only to rehire the skills on a contract basis.

**Work...**
...is changing with power, authority and initiative occurring much further down the organisation requiring more rapid development earlier in careers and at every level. Creativity and innovation are in demand and much more likely at the younger end of the organisation. The fewer managers have to delegate to cope and the lower number of promotional positions means new methods of measuring and rewarding contribution are needed. As more and more work is short-term contract and more people work on a temporary consulting basis, new skills of self- reliance, self -development and self-selling are added to the basic skills.

**Learning**

Attitudes, approaches and demands with regard to learning are also changing. It has proved surprisingly difficult to transfer academic learning into work requirements. Students, graduates and employers are frequently highly critical of degrees. The focus has alighted on learning at work and research into ways of learning has produced new insights with mentoring itself recognised as a direct facilitator with impressive results for behaviour change.

## 3. Mentoring Process

A simple process requiring subtlety for effectiveness.

A relationship of trust and confidentiality, openness and honesty is now possible.

Goals are established by questioning and checking.

Current reality is agreed.

New goals and possibilities are explored. New goals are evaluated and selected. Actions are planned to achieve.

Skills are developed to facilitate the above.

Repeat, concentrating always on learning abilities of the learner, their independence and ability to help themselves.

## Why mentoring?

- Mentoring is particularly useful in modern conditions of change and uncertainty. It focuses learning and development within the workplace and supports acquisition of continuous learning and personal development applied at the level of the individual, by an individual.

- Mentoring is a natural process which benefits greatly by formalising it and training mentors.

- Research shows mentoring is the process with the most potential as a learning method.

- Mentoring benefits all levels including the organisation and the mentor.

- Research into adult/professional development showed very strong influence on achievement in having and being a mentor.

- American success with mentoring programmes to aid the socially disadvantaged in the workplace propelled mentoring into being a major process for handling change and developing people.

# Characteristics of Mentoring

1. It uniquely focuses the learner on their potential and it's achievement by their own efforts.

2. It is a one-to-one personal relationship of trust, confidentiality and adult-to-adult.

3. It is concerned with feelings, motives, needs and interests rather than technical, instructional adequacy.

4. Constant feedback and reflection by an impartial but concerned and experienced individual has no counterpart in other development methods.

5. It is preferably off-line of command and control which allows complete honesty and removes role conflicts.

6. It is highly flexible permitting accommodation of any circumstances and people's characteristics.

7. It operates exceptionally well in the workplace using ongoing experience as the development vehicle.

8. It does not require choice between mentoring and other activities.

9. It is generally low in cost and resources in the context of professional development.

10. It is beneficial to all sections and persons in an organisation.

11. It is part of a learning culture which is the modern necessity for adaptation and survival in a rapid change environment.

12. It is seldom damaging even if not expertly performed.

13. It stresses the independence and responsibility of the learner for their own development by not being directive.

14. Ideally, it is not recognised that the mentor is also in a learning situation.

15. The business of mentoring is learning and the mentor/learner relationship is a learning alliance.

# 4. Mentor Characteristics

## Positive

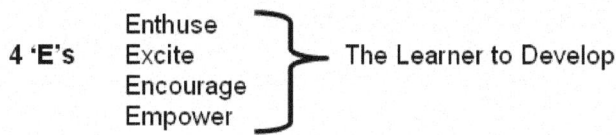

- Ability to respond to learner's individuality
- Mental energy
- Action – orientated
- Professional reputation
- Networker and facilitator
- Sound and broad knowledge of organisation
- Learner
- Listener, coach, counsellor
- Interpreter of objectives
- Mutually trustful and respectful
- Able to operate adult-to-adult with learner.
- Literate and lucid
- Accessible

## Negative

- Heavily committed to other projects
- Inaccessible, elusive, aloof
- Newly in post.
- Involved in corporate politics
- Own staff have poor morale
- Too distant in level in organisation
- Poor communicator/interviewer
- Non-learner
- Rigid personality

# Notes on 'wise counsellor'

'Counselling' is the heart of mentoring with its focus on the learner aided to develop themselves within a confidential, trusting, one-to-one off-line relationship.

'Wise', however, is difficult to use in the modern world.

Some comments from Dr. De Bono's
'Textbook of Wisdom', however, could be very pertinent for mentors and the mentoring process.

## 'Wisdom'

*'Wisdom is the art with which perception crafts experience to serve our values'.*

Wisdom is **not** cleverness.

Wisdom is more **perspective** than detail. Wisdom takes place in the area of broader, deeper, richer **perception**.

Wisdom is about **usefulness**.

Wisdom is to think slowly and **avoid habitual patterns**.

Wisdom is the ability to **see through** surface appearance.

Wisdom concerns **perception** and thinking of possibilities, then creating and generating alternatives.

Wisdom demands the use of **creativity**. Wisdom is a matter of **awareness andchoice** and choice of a direction to makesome effort.

Wisdom is the **operating system** of perception.

**Contribution gets rid of boredom. Invest in interest.**

There is a **joy in achievement**.

## Key Points

1. **RAPID CHANGE** demands changes in people, skills, organisations, attitudes and processes.

2. **LEARNING-TO-LEARN** is the key skill in successful adaptation to change.

3. **MENTORING IS THE MOST EFFECTIVE METHOD** of facilitating learning.

4. **MENTORING BENEFITS ALL.**

## 5.    Roles

1. Organisation

2. Organiser/Administrator

3. Line Manager/Supervisor

4. Mentor

5. Trainee/Learner

# 'ORGANISATION'

**AIMS**   Requirements for viability and success
Challenges to be met

**INPUT**   Initiatives and changes in structure VISIBLE Board
Commitment to professional excellence
Information on present position and future targets
Resources for professional development

**OUTPUTS**   Competently trained regulators
Contribution during training
Learning Organisation
Culture Change
Adaptable responsive organisation
Competitiveness

**BENEFITS**

- Increased departmental interaction

- Staff aspirations satisfied

- Learning culture – adaptable company

- Change more readily assured

- More capable staff

- Better recruitment possibilities

- Attract and retain quality staff

# 'ORGANISER / ADMINSTRATOR'

*(Usually Personnel/Training)*

**AIMS**     Implement organisation aims

**INPUT**     Initiate and administer programme including external secondments
Demonstrate VISIBLE high level backing
Obtain all-round support from all parties
Organise trainee placements and backup resources
Monitor scheme for success and contribution
Manage induction for a flying start
Ensure that company and learner/trainee goals are compatible
Help select mentors

**OUTPUT**     Successful learner/trainee progress and achievement
Company obtains employees capable of adding value
Employees capable of meeting company's competitive challenges
Line managers recognise training/development value
Attractive recruitment profile

## 'LINE MANAGER / SUPERVISOR'

**AIM**     Develops employee capable of adding value
Provides development opportunities for trainee/learner aspirations

**INPUT**     Teaching special skills
Assessment and feedback of trainee performance
Demonstrates professional/company excellence
Uses trainee as a valuable resource
Adapts assignments to achieve both task and learning objectives
Offers tacit support to mentor as a valuable resource
Places expectation on trainee to fully utilise mentor resource
Co-operates with mentor at latter's induction with trainee
Openly expects trainee to negotiate learning opportunities

**OUTPUT**     Trainee contribution to department
Company used as a learning vehicle
Rapid achievement of company and trainee objectives
Quality employee with demonstrable externally assessed qualifications
Improved departmental and company image
More competitive culture

**BENEFITS**

- Improve staff competency
- Reduces training costs
- Increased productivity
- Reduced turnover of young professionals
- Rapid transfer of experience
- Reduced labour/recruitment costs
- Faster induction
- Improved cross-functional co-operation

# 'COACH'

**AIM**  Counsel trainee to achieve rapid increased employability via professional achievement

**INPUT**  Confidential counselling to develop trainee personality
Professional role model
Skilled mentoring demonstrating full breadth of professional characteristics
Manage the relationship not the trainee.
Interpret goals and methods
Coach to fully exploit all assignments
Evaluation and feedback are given to trainee
Learning for self
Knowledge of programme requirements
Accent on learners/trainees independence and responsibilities

**OUTPUT**  Self-development and learning
Updating and self-analysis. Input to profession
Career enhancement
Satisfaction of aiding a trainee / learner
Reinforcement of own professionalism
New look at the profession
New insights and perceptions
Job enrichment
Movement across company boundaries
Addition to mentor's CV

## BENEFITS

- Development of mentoring skills for personal CV
- Job enrichment in developing others
- Personal learning
- Putting back into the profession
- Exposure to new attitudes/insights/perceptions
- Status/professional recognition
- Psychic rewards
- Career enhancement
- Technical updating
- Movement across departmental boundaries
- CPD

## 'Trainee / Learner'

**AIM**   Rapid personal and professional development to achieve optimum employability

**INPUT**   Commitment to appropriate objectives
Owns training career and life
Develops ability to use mentor as a valuable resource
Seeks responsibility and independence
Understands the programme and its requirements
Manages self as a prerequisite for managing others
Chooses a profession rather than a job
Concentrates on employability rather than on employment
Commitment to continuous learning
Pursues creative opportunities & innovative thinking
Identifies criteria for professional & company portfolio building
Develops skills of evidence collection & portfolio building

**OUTPUT**   Early achievement of professional competence
Employability and early access to good opportunities
Streetwise with technical, commercial and interpersonal skills
Ability to market self

**BENEFITS**

- Learning-to-learn
- Opportunity to learn from experienced professionals
- Access to the intangible aspects of professionalism
- Access to learning and development opportunities
- Counselling using work as the major development vehicle
- Feedback from an impartial source
- Maximising opportunities
- Networking and career-orientation
- Early contribution
- Introduction to politics of the workplace
- Expanded vision
- Exposure to senior management

## 6. Pitfalls

- Creation of elite
- Resentment if progress closed off to others
- Mentor cloning or too directive
- Undermining of line authority
- Meandering if no clear goals set
- Operating in vacuum if no high level backing
- Task demands overwhelm learning objectives
- Politics and culture (e.g. non graduate)
- Bad chemistry between mentor and learner
- Dependency
- Conflict of roles if manager is mentor
- Learner not committed

# 7. Learning Styles Questionnaire

This questionnaire is designed to help you to identify your preferred learning style, so that you are in a better position to select learning experiences that suit your style and to identify different learning styles in others.

You should be as honest as possible. There are no right or wrong answers. If you agree more than you disagree with the statement put a tick by it. If you disagree more than you agree put a cross by it. Be sure to mark each item with either a tick or a cross.

1. [ ] I have strong beliefs about what is right and wrong, good and bad.
2. [ ] I often "throw caution to the winds"
3. [ ] I tend to solve problems using a step-by-step approach, avoiding any "flights-of-fancy".
4. [ ] I believe that formal procedures and policies cramp people's style.
5. [ ] I have a reputation for having no-nonsense, "I call a spade a spade".
6. [ ] I often find that actions base on 'gut feel' are as sound as those based on careful thought and analysis.
7. [ ] I like to do the sort of work where I have time to "leave no stone unturned".
8. [ ] I regularly question people about their basic assumptions.
9. [ ] What matters most is whether something works in practice.
10. [ ] I actively seek out new experiences.
11. [ ] When I hear about a new idea or approach, I immediately start working out how to apply it in practice.

12. [ ]  I am keen on self-discipline such as watching my diet, taking regular exercise, sticking to a fixed routine.
13. [ ]  I take pride in doing a thorough job.
14. [ ]  I get on best with logical, analytical people and less well with spontaneous, 'irrational' people.
15. [ ]  I take care over the interpretation of data available to me and avoid jumping conclusions.
16. [ ]  I like to reach a decision carefully after weighing up many alternatives.
17. [ ]  I'm attracted more to novel, unusual ideas than to practical ones.
18. [ ]  I don't like 'loose ends' and prefer to fit things into a coherent pattern.
19. [ ]  I accept and stick to laid down procedures and policies so long as I regard them as an efficient way of getting the job done.
20. [ ]  I like to relate my actions to a general principle.
21. [ ]  In discussions I like to get straight to the point.
22. [ ]  I tend to have distant, rather formal relationships with people at work.
23. [ ]  I thrive on the challenge of tackling something new and different.
24. [ ]  I enjoy fun-loving, spontaneous people.
25. [ ]  I pay meticulous attention to detail before coming to a decision.
26. [ ]  I find it difficult to come up with wild, off-the-head ideas.
27. [ ]  I don't believe in wasting time by "beating around the bush".
28. [ ]  I am careful not to jump to conclusions too quickly.
29. [ ]  I prefer to have as many sources of information as possible – the more to mull over the better.

30. [ ]  Flippant people who don't take things seriously enough usually irritate me.
31. [ ]  I listen to other people's point of view before putting my own forward.
32. [ ]  I tend to be open about how I am feeling.
33. [ ]  In discussions I enjoy the manoeuvring of other participants.
34. [ ]  I prefer to respond to events on a spontaneous, flexible basis rather than plan things out in advance.
35. [ ]  I tend to be attracted to techniques such as network analysis, flow charts, branching programmes, contingency planning etc.
36. [ ]  It worries me if I have to rush out a piece of work to meet a tight deadline.
37. [ ]  I tend to judge people's ideas on their practical merits.
38. [ ]  Quiet, thoughtful people tend to make me feel uneasy.
39. [ ]  I often get irritated by people who want to rush headlong into things.
40. [ ]  It is more important to enjoy the present moment than to think about the past or future.
41. [ ]  I think that decisions based on a thorough analysis of all information are sounder than those based on intuition.
42. [ ]  I tend to be a perfectionist.
43. [ ]  In discussions I usually pitch in with lots of off-the-top of-the-head ideas.
44. [ ]  In meetings I put forward practical realistic ideas.
45. [ ]  More often than not, rules are there to be broken.
46. [ ]  I prefer to stand back from a situation and consider all the perspectives.
47. [ ]  I can often see inconsistencies and weaknesses in other people's arguments.
48. [ ]  On balance I talk more than I listen.

http://www.map-int.com

49. [ ] I can often see better, more practical ways to get things done.
50. [ ] I think written reports should be short, punchy and to the point.
51. [ ] I believe that rational, logical thinking should win the day.
52. [ ] I tend to discuss specific things with people rather than engaging in "small talk"
53. [ ] I like people who have both feet firmly on the ground.
54. [ ] In discussions I get impatient with irrelevancies and "red herrings".
55. [ ] If I have a report to write, I tend to produce lots of drafts before settling on the final version.
56. [ ] I am keen to try things out to see if they work in practice.
57. [ ] I am keen to reach answers via a logical approach.
58. [ ] I enjoy being the one that talks a lot.
59. [ ] In discussions I often find I am the realist, keeping people to the point and avoiding "cloud nine" speculations.
60. [ ] I like to ponder many alternatives before making up my mind.
61. [ ] In discussions with people I often find I am the most dispassionate and objective.
62. [ ] In discussions I'm more likely to adopt a "low profile" than to take the lead and do most of the talking.
63. [ ] I like to be able to relate current actions to a longer term bigger picture.
64. [ ] When things go wrong I am happy to shrug it off and "put it down to experience".
65. [ ] I tend to reject wild, off-the-top-of-the-head ideas as being impractical.
66. [ ] It is best to "look before you leap"
67. [ ] On balance I do the listening rather than the talking.

68. [ ]   I tend to be tough on people who find it difficult to adopt a logical approach.
69. [ ]   Most times I believe the end justifies the means.
70. [ ]   I don't mind hurting people's feelings so long as the job gets done.
71. [ ]   I find the formality of having specific objectives and plans stifling.
72. [ ]   I'm usually the "life and soul of the party".
73. [ ]   I do whatever is expedient to get the job done.
74. [ ]   I quickly get bored with methodical, detailed work.
75. [ ]   I am keen on exploring the basic assumptions, principles and theories underpinning things and events.
76. [ ]   I'm always interested to find out what other people think.
77. [ ]   I like meetings to be run on methodical lines, sticking to laid down agenda, etc.
78. [ ]   I steer clear of subjective or ambiguous topics.
79. [ ]   I enjoy the drama and excitement of a crisis situation.
80. [ ]   People often find me insensitive to their feelings.

# Scoring

You score one point for each item you ticked. There are no points for the items out crossed.

Simply indicate on the list below which items were ticked

| 2 | 7 | 1 | 5 |
| 4 | 13 | 3 | 9 |
| 6 | 15 | 8 | 11 |
| 10 | 16 | 12 | 19 |
| 17 | 25 | 14 | 21 |
| 23 | 28 | 18 | 27 |
| 24 | 29 | 20 | 35 |
| 32 | 31 | 22 | 37 |
| 34 | 33 | 26 | 44 |
| 38 | 36 | 30 | 49 |
| 40 | 39 | 42 | 50 |
| 43 | 41 | 47 | 53 |
| 45 | 46 | 51 | 54 |
| 48 | 52 | 57 | 56 |
| 58 | 55 | 61 | 59 |
| 64 | 60 | 63 | 65 |
| 71 | 62 | 68 | 69 |
| 72 | 66 | 75 | 70 |
| 74 | 67 | 77 | 73 |
| 79 | 76 | 78 | 80 |

Totals

| Activist | Reflector | Theorist | Pragmatist |

http://www.map-int.com

# Learning Styles Analysis

## Active (Activist)

- Gets involved in new experiences
- Open-minded
- Will "try anything once"
- Very active
- Likes to be "fire-fighting"
- Gets bored implementing and "fine-tuning"
- Gets highly involved in group situations

**Learns best from activities where:**

- There are new experiences/problems/opportunities to learn from.

- He/she can become engrossed in short "here and now" activities such as business games competitive teamwork tasks, role plays.

- There is excitement/drama/crisis and things chop and change with a range of diverse activities to tackle.

- He/she is allowed to generate ideas without constraints of policy or structure or feasibility.

- He/she has a lot of limelight/high visibility, e.g. chairing meetings, leading discussions, giving presentations.

- He/she is thrown in at the deep end with a task he/she thinks is difficult e.g. when set a challenge with inadequate resources and adverse conditions.

- He/she is involved with other people, bouncing ideas off them, solving problems as part of a team.

- It is appropriate to "have a go"

**Learns least from, and may react against, activities where:**

- Learning involves a passive role, e.g. listening to lectures, monologues, explanations, statements of how things should be done, reading and watching.

- He/she is asked to stand back and not be involved.

- He/she is required to assimilate, analyse and interpret lots of "messy" data.

- He/she is required to engage in solitary work, e.g. reading, writing.

- He/she is asked to assess beforehand what he/she will learn, and to appraise learning afterwards.

- He/she is offered statements he/she sees as "theoretical", e.g. explanations of cause or background.

- He/she is asked to repeat essentially the same activity over and over i.e. when practising.

- He/she has precise instructions to follow with little room for manoeuvre.

- He/she is asked to do a thorough job i.e. attend to detail, tie up loose ends.

# Thinking (Reflector)

- Stands back and "chews over" new experiences.
- Likes to collect information rather than reach decisions.
- Thoughtful
- Cautious
- Takes a back seat in group situations
- Likes to hear others' views before voicing own

**Learns best from activities where:**

- He/she is allowed or encouraged to watch/think/chew over activities.

- He/she is able to stand back from events and listen/observe e.g. observing a group at work, taking a back seat at a meeting, watching a film.

- He/she is allowed to think before acting, to assimilate before commenting, e.g. has time to prepare, a chance to read in advance a brief giving background data.

- He/she can carry out some painstaking research, e.g. investigate, and assemble information, probe to get to the bottom of things.

- He/she has the opportunity to review carefully considered analyses and reports.

- He/she is helped to exchange views with other people without danger, i.e. by prior agreement, within a structured learning experience.

- He/she can reach a decision in his/her own time, without pressure and tight deadlines.

**Learns least from, and may react against activities where:**

- He/she is forced into the limelight, e.g. to act as leader/chairman, to role play in front of others.

- He/she is involved in situations which require action without planning.

- He/she is pitched into doing something without warning, i.e. to produce an instant reaction, to produce an off-the-top-of-the-head idea.

- He/she is given insufficient data on which to base a conclusion.

- He/she is given cut and dried instructions of how things should be done.

- He/she is worried by time pressures or rushed from one activity to another.

- In the interests of expediency, he/she has to make short cuts or do a superficial job.

# Logical (Theorist)

- Works through new situations step by step
- Likes to "make things fit"
- Perfectionist
- Uncomfortable with making judgements
- Lateral thinker

**Learns best from activities where:**

- What is being offered is part of a system, model, concept, theory.

- He/she has time to explore methodically the associations and interrelationships between ideas, events and situations.

- He/she has the chance to question and probe basic methodology, assumptions or logic behind something e.g. by taking part in a question and answer session, by checking a paper for inconsistencies.

- He/she is intellectually stretched, e.g. by analysing a complex situation, being tested in a tutorial session, by teaching high calibre people who ask searching questions.

- He/she is in structured situations with clear purpose.

- He/she can listen to or read about ideas and concepts that emphasise rationally or logic and are well argued/elegant/watertight.

- He/she can analyse and then generalise the reasons for success or failure.

- He/she is offered interesting ideas and concepts even though they are not immediately relevant.

- He/she is required to understand and participate in complex situations.

## Learn least from, and may react against activities where:

- He/she is pitch-forked into doing something without a context or apparent purpose.

- He/she has to participate in situations emphasising emotions and feelings.

- He/she is involved in unstructured activities where ambiguity and uncertainty are high, e.g. with open-ended problems, on sensitivity training.

- He/she is asked to act or decide without a basis in policy, principle or concept.

- He/she is faced with a hotchpotch of alternative/contradictory techniques/methods without exploring any depth.

- He/she doubts that the subject matter is methodically sound e.g. where questionnaires haven't been validated, where there aren't any statistics to support an argument.

- He/she finds the subject matter platitudinous, shallow or gimmicky.

- He/she feels out of tune with other participants, e.g. when with lots of activists or people of lower intellectual calibre.

# Practical (Pragmatists)

- Keen to try out new ideas to see if they work
- Looks for new ideas
- Experiments
- Comes back from courses bubbling with new ideas to try
- Does not like lengthy discussions on new ideas
- Makes decisions and gets on with them
- Problems are challenges
- Always sees a better way of doing things

**Learns best from activities where:**

- There is an obvious link between the subject matter and a problem or opportunity on the job.

- He/she is shown techniques for doing things with obvious practical advantages, e.g. how to save time, how to make a good first impression, deal with awkward people.

- He/she has the chance to try out and practice techniques with coaching/feedback from a credible expert, e.g. someone who is successful and can do the techniques themselves.

- He/she is exposed to a model he/she can emulate, e.g. a respected boss, a demonstration from someone with a proven track record, lots of examples/anecdotes, a film showing how it is done.

- He/she is given techniques currently applicable to his/her own job.

- He/she is given immediate opportunities to implement what has been learned.

- There is high face validity in the learning activity, e.g. good simulation, real problems.

- He/she can concentrate on practical issues, e.g. drawing up action plans with an obvious end product, suggesting short cuts, giving tips.

**Learns least from, and may react against activities where:**

- The learning is not related to an immediate need or where he/she cannot see an immediate relevance/practical benefit.

- Organisers of the learning, or the event itself, seem distant from reality e.g. "ivory towered", all theory and general principles, pure "chalk and talk".

- There is no practice or clear guidelines on how to do it.

- He/she feels that people are going round in circles and not getting anywhere fast enough.

- There are political, managerial or personal obstacles to implementation.

- He/she cannot see sufficient reward from the learning activity, e.g. more sales, shorter meetings, higher bonus, promotion.

# PART 2

# EXPLORATION of MENTORING PRACTICE

## 1. Learning Cycle and Styles

**LEARNING....** is a relatively permanent change in behaviour resulting from practice and repetition

Mentors will need to take learner's confidence into account, especially at the start, as it will affect the learners ability to set high but achievable goals, take responsibility for their own learning and generally become more independent. How people learn becomes important knowledge for mentors as this guides their intervention when promoting learning and maximising such opportunities from work activities.

## 2. Kolb's Learning Cycle

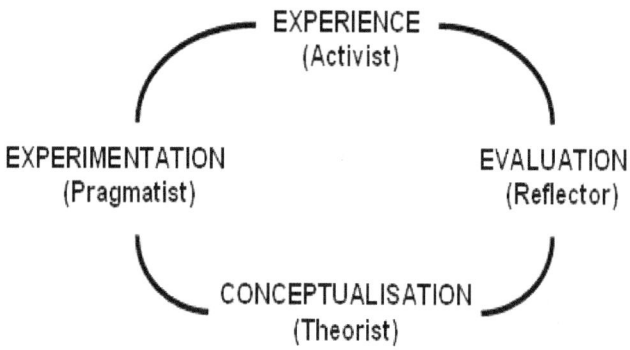

This cyclical process involves questions, challenges and checks at all stages of an activity and guides mentors to intervene to move people round the cycle.

### It consists of:

**Experience**      Mentor assists learner to structure and organise their experience by judicious questioning.

What, how, why etc. powerfully influence the learner to be specific.

| | |
|---|---|
| Evaluation | Mentor encourages learner to focus on explicit experiences and to review their significance. Reflection is a basic need for learning to take place. |
| | What, why, how etc. again aid focusing and understanding. |
| Conceptualisation | Mentor encourages learner to make sense of experiences and fit them into a wider context by generalising and modelling, seeking patterns, systems and processes rather than mere events. |
| | Questioning is again extremely powerful. |
| Experimentation | From effective modelling, prediction should be encouraged. Here trial testing produces a reality-check and encourages identifying future tasks and learning objectives. |
| | Questioning again plays its part. |

**Such simple but perceptive questioning benefits by:**

1. Moving people into the next stage and around the cycle.

2. Developing self-awareness as the learner becomes aware of the learning cycle and which stage they are more comfortable with.

3. Capturing the learning potential of any situation

# Using Kolb's Learning Cycle

## Experience

An activity that may be planned or accidental, failure or success, courses or work. Mentor input is to help structure the activity, by insisting on specific and measurable objective setting by the trainee/learner.

## Evaluation

Reflection and observation on experience to establish understanding. Mentor input is to act as a focuser by insisting on explicit attention to various aspects of the experience.

## Conceptualisation

Analysis and generalisation to establish a theory of the experience allowing predictions in similar circumstances. Mentor input is to encourage trainee to model experience by seeking explanations, pattern, cause – effect chains and feedback loops.

# Experimentation

Theories must be tested by trials and predictions in future experience, thus closing the cycle. Mentor input is to reveal that the reality check occurs when trainee's new ideas, forecasts, predictions and new aims and objectives are realistic. Task and learning objectives must be identified.

**Note**

1. Questions, checks and challenges follow at any stage of learning to impel movements around the cycle and extract maximum progress from experience.

2. Mentors find the subtle use of questions the most powerful form of influential intervention whilst avoiding direction.

# Learning Styles - Summary

The above process is likely to reveal learner preference for a particular style, though generally not to the exclusion of other stages. Whichever stage is preferred can also imply preference for a particular learning style.

The four styles have strengths and weaknesses summarised below:

**Activists**  Prefer 'experience' stage of problems and challenges and are comfortable in high profile activities.

Learn best with present action activities and stress situations and interaction with other people.

Learn least in a positive role, in solitary activities and in absorbing high volumes of data.

**Reflectors**  Prefer time to think and mull over various alternatives. As they listen and watch they are generally low profile.

Learn best if given thinking time, if given all relevant information and if action is not needed quickly.

Learn least if under pressure, with inadequate information and when forced into the limelight.

**Theorists** — Assimilate and synthesise information into structures and explanatory systems. They are strong on principles, assumptions and reasoning, fitting new data into their complex schemes and objecting to subjectivity.

Learn best: using coherent systems or models, when able to explore connections etc. between facts and ideas, if subject matter is coherent.

Learn least if purpose is not evident, if no time is given to establish coherent base and if context is emotive.

**Pragmatists** — Value new experiences to see how they actually work. They are practical and enjoy problem solving and getting on with the job.

Learn best when dealing with practical activities, when getting stuck in how and when result is likely to be of use.

Learn least when overwhelmed by theory, when no practical use is in sight and when the activity is divorced from practical use.

## Using Learning Styles and Cycle

Mentor and learner should become aware of their own and others preferences as both are learners and style significantly affect learning confidence. Mentor, however, must
encourage learner through all learning stages to widen their skills base and develop their learning potential, as all stages are interdependent, and no one stage must be ignored.

If mentor and learner have the same or different learning styles mutual awareness creates powerful learning potential for both if they share knowledge. Listening, questioning and feedback can trigger new vision and learning in both.

# 3. Skills for Mentoring

*'Giving Attention'*

…as a basic **communication necessity** by:

- Obviously listening rather than being distracted.
- Using a range of non-verbal signals (body language) to reinforce item 1.
- Making eye contact but only to a reassuring degree.
- Body positioning that indicates a relaxed atmosphere.
- Facial expression reflecting what is being discussed.
- Nodding, smiling, doing small sounds showing concentration and understanding and encourages trainee to proceed.
- Not interrupting learner is to do most talking.
- Allowing occasional silence to avoid pressurising the trainee and provide thinking time.

## *'Interpersonal skills'*

...to develop trust!

1. Acceptance of people as they are:

    **DO**    Show respect, express empathy, be genuine

    **DO NOT**    Be condescending or judgmental


2. Appreciation of person separate from the problem.

Problem Solving:

    **DO**    Question with focus on the problem not the person

    **DO NOT**    Seek to blame or accept generalisations, vagueness and evaluations without question

Clarifying:

    **DO**    Guide from general to specific, vague to concrete

    **DO NOT**    Jump to conclusions or ask multiple questions

Summarising:

**DO**         Check conclusions and agree on objectives

**DO NOT**     Use jargon, mumble or ramble on

3. Showing interest and involvement

**DO**         Listen – see prompt attend to verbal and non- verbal responses

Be open and reflective

Focus questions or comments on what was said

Confront inconsistencies and incongruities

**DO NOT**     Appear bored, hostile or impatient.

Check watch or interrupt.

Change conversation abruptly, preventing elaboration or further exploration by Trainee

Ask closed questions

Accept inconsistencies

Make unchecked assumptions and interpretations

4. Conveying Understanding

  **DO**  Playback and reflect what Trainee has said, focus on feelings

  **DO NOT**  Jump to the conclusions. Reflect back what Trainee has said

5. Being Genuine

  **DO**  Disclose information about oneself

    Give honest, appropriate feedback

    STRESS confidentiality

    Have reputation for keeping confidences.

  **DO NOT**  Project conflicting verbal and non-verbal messages

    Be judgemental

    Cite other cases using named exemplars

## 'Listening'

Effective *LISTENING* by the mentor is both highly instrumental in developing the relationship and interviews plus being highly prized by the trainees. It is far more than just hearing and requires communicating to the trainee. Perceptive listening interacts closely with appropriate questioning and their contribution allows exploration of the trainees' point of view.

## Active listening

...is very demanding and has several stages:

- Reflective feelings involved in the discussion by responding to their tone, volume, facial expressions etc.

- Paraphrase by restating what they say but in a different way to check that you understand and encourage further discussion. Question any points that are unclear.

- Summarise and reflect content, feelings and implications to now serve as a springboard to extend the discussion into new territory.

- Interpret the key points raised by the speaker into a coherent focus for developing action alternatives.

- Target the trainee talking at least two thirds of the time.

<u>Impediments</u> to active listening are:

- Distractions of all kinds.
- Physical barriers of space, accessibility, lack of quiet room.
- Hearing only what we expect to hear.
- Unchecked assumptions.
- Too much detail; trainee cannot précis.
- Selective listening, filtering out unwelcome views.
- Emotive language, which interferes with thinking.
- No agenda and discussion rambles.
- Boredom if discussion is outside our narrow interests.
- Competition with the trainee. Interruptions show the competitive non-listener.
- Closed mind. Prejudice inhibits intelligence, preventing thinking.

## *'Questioning'*

Appropriate questions assist in building the relationship, demonstrate attention and structure discussions so they remain targeted and relevant and lead the trainee into new perceptions/perspectives.

Different types of questions serve different functions requiring skill in selection. They are basically closed or open.

CLOSED questions, which demands:

    A) Yes or No answer,
       Or
    B) Specific Information,

…and do not allow further discussion. They are useful when trying to clarify specifics and deciding actions. However the **control stays with the questioner** and too many invoke a third degree atmosphere. They have their place but only with deliberation.

OPEN questions are used to:

    A) Establish rapport
    B) Explore broad background
    C) Reveal opinions, attitudes and feelings.

Their great asset is that they leave the questioned in control, facilitating co-operation, trust and confidence and having feelings and circumstances respected.

Question types are analysed in greater depth on the following page.

# Types of Questions

**Closed**  A question which leads to a specific answer, often requiring only one or two words for answer.

A closed question should only be used when specific, factual information is being sought. It is not designed to encourage discussion, expression of opinion or debate.

Be aware of the stilted effect closed questions can produce and only use them when you want a direct, unambiguous response.

EXAMPLES: "How many years have you worked here?", "Do you enjoy your job?", "Have you applied for promotion?"

**Open**  A question which leaves the person being questioned free to respond in a way which suits them and allows them to have control over the information they impart.

Open questions are very important for gaining a detailed view of what the individual thinks, wants, expects, feels, etc. They do not constrain the individual by setting limits to the scope of the question.

EXAMPLES: "Tell me about your last job", "What aspects of this particular project appeal to you?", "What kind of job would you like to see yourself doing in five years' time?"

**Probing**

These are questions which explore a bit more deeply than simple open questions

EXAMPLES: "So, what specifically could you do to achieve your goal?" "What arguments did you use to persuade Finance to fund the project?")

Probing questions may need to be used to "pin down" just exactly what it is a person is aiming at, what precise, practical steps they need to take next or what specific assistance they require from you.

**Leading**

These are questions that suggest, by the way they are asked or phrased, that a specific answer is required or expected

By their nature, leading questions often receive short precise answers like closed questions. This is because the questioner is trying to "lead" the individual to a particular answer or conclusion.

Be wary of using these types of questions to put your ideas into someone else's head.
Try not to direct in this way, but use open and probing questions to make the individual think for him/herself.

EXAMPLES: "I suppose you would prefer to stay in my department for the rest of your training?" "Most people find it difficult to understand Mr X's lectures – don't you?"

**Reflecting**   These 'reflect' back to the speaker what he/she has said

Reflecting questions should be used to play back to the speaker what you have heard and to clarify the points covered.

They give the individual the opportunity to correct any misunderstanding or to ensure the right emphasis is given to particular points.

EXAMPLES: "So you think you would prefer open learning rather than going back to college?" "You've suggested that the new planning system would be acceptable to everyone, is that right?"

## 'Objective-setting'

Experience has shown that, all too often, set objectives are 'soft', such as 'appreciation' and 'understanding' etc., and tend to either be demanding to the trainee or to focus on professional contribution; in particular there is failure to require an innovator response. An additional hazard is 'drift', with discussions and meetings not resulting in actions.

As an aid to improving this situation, remember:

## SMART

**S**pecific — Keep objectives simple and concise so that both mentor and learner are clear what they are.

**M**easurable — This allows both parties to identify whether or not objectives are wholly or partly achieved. It is an essential skill for professional regulators.

**Appropriate** Aim for targets that are attainable, though with some stretch.

**Realistic** Related to the company business, the objectives are a real contribution.

**Timely** The opportunities of the moment are seized, rather than following a rigid formula. Objectives also suit the stage of development.

## 'Facilitating'

Is the process of enabling things to happen and is a key skill for a professional to have and pass to learner. Good managers do this all the time but the special relevance for mentors is to ensure learners are exposed to the full range of experience they need but the task of the job may not provide.

**Core skills are:** Clarification of goals and needs of the learner and their aspirations.

Recognition of barriers and impediments, which may also be in the mind and personality of the learner.

Counselling and guiding learner to overcome impediments. Ease the learner's path if necessary by networking.

Lack of understanding of 'politics' may be the major impediment.

## 'Networking'

The process of obtaining value from informal channels. Generally a natural unobserved activity, it becomes an explicit skill when its benefits are understood and deliberately sought.

Critical decisions at all levels, personal and otherwise, are frequently made in this way. Companies rarely function as the organisation chart displays. It is so important that it should be explicitly recognised and developed by mentor and trainee alike.

Great care must be taken to distinguish use from abuse and to be aware of the political nature of some of these involvements.

**Core skills are:** Explicit recognition of its existence, value and potential.

Defining what it is and its characteristics. Influence and mutual benefit replace authority connections. Identify key areas to reach and likely long and short term values to be obtained.

### Develop networks

By developing approaches and interpersonal skills for reaching these key areas. Create alliances and trade-offs.

Know how and when to use them. Interpersonal skills are crucial. A strong appreciation of 'politics' and what you can offer as well as gain is essential. What the appeal is to other parties requires a subtle appreciation of personality traits and psychology of people.

# 'Feedback'

Feedback is a way of learning more about ourselves and the effect our behaviour has on others.

Constructive feedback increases self- awareness, offers options and encourages development. Skilfully done negative as well as positive feedback can be valuable. Unskilled feedback demoralises without providing learning options; recipient must be left with choice.

## Giving Skilled Feedback

1. **Start with the positive**; the negatives are more likely to be listened to.

2. **Be specific,** it provides more learning opportunities.

3. **Offer alternatives** when offering a negative comment, so that it then becomes a positive suggestion. Leave recipient with choice.

4. **Describe not evaluate**, avoidance of a judgemental attitude is essential.

5. **It is your feedback**, not a universal opinion, so use 'I' and it becomes entirely your responsibility.

6. **Examine** the consequences of the choices for change you have suggested.

## *'Coaching'*

Coaching, in this context is assignment specific, where the mentor assists the trainee to set objectives that extract the maximum learning opportunities from that experience, with the aim of developing their performance.

Assistance is also given by surrounding their activity with questions; observations and comments that make the learner focus on the quality of their ongoing performance.

Feedback on the state of their knowledge, attitude and skill all combine to focus their attention on:

- Planning
- Self-awareness
- Attitude and confidence
- Monitoring and self-assessment Adaptability
- Thinking to offer observations and improvements

Coaching intervention must be careful to leave the initiative with the learner, but some structure and direction will still allow spontaneous learning.

The '3 Ds' structure of:

**Define**  First the general aim, and then narrow to specific goals using SMART. The skills of listening and open and closed questions operate here.

**Describe**  This shows the current reality for the learner and the facts, figures, processes, attitudes, circumstances etc., the learner is aware of. **Feedback** skills operate here. Necessary changes now surface and this is the purpose of this stage.

**Decide**  Generate and evaluate options possibilities and alternatives, then learner decides action. Coaching assists learner to overcome attitude/confidence impediments.

Practice and evaluate periodically so this 3 stage process becomes a continuous cycle working on the personality of the learner receiving continuous feedback, monitoring etc. that keeps a clear focus on learning progression.

http://www.map-int.com

Coaching calls for the mentor to show:

- A) A desire to see the learner develop

- B) The ability to keep the initiative always with the learner whilst still influencing them to make their appropriate decisions.

- C) A continuous focus on learning.

**Key skills used are:**
- Listening
- Questioning
- Coaching '3Ds'
- Feedback
- Challenging
- Monitoring
- Structuring
- Experience
- Setting Goals – SMART

## 'Counselling'

The heart of mentoring is counselling, often defined as:

*"Helping another person explore and understand their own potential and assisting them in developing it to the full"*

*"It is a relationship rather than an activity and requires mutual trust and confidentiality and is off-line, adult-to-adult if it is to be effective"*

Typical characteristics that distinguish counselling from coaching are:

A) NOT primarily about operational matters.

B) NOT about performance or competence.

C) Involves problems, difficulties, impediments, frustrations and relationships.

D) Involves deep personal levels including emotions, hopes, fears, values etc. that are having a negative impact. Change is required but can be threatening and is never trivial.

The same '3Ds' used in coaching are a useful structure but application and intervention are different:

**Define**  Challenge to find out what is wanted. Insist on specifics to enable negative complaints to be moved to positive statements that now allow structure and purpose to the discussion. The climate must be set for complete honesty to surface.

**Describe**  Explore by allowing learner to talk about feelings and emotions as well as facts. Both mentor and learner must become aware of the basic dimensions of the problem. The learner's self- awareness and personal disclosures allows the mentor to judge the learner's accuracy and comprehensives of understanding of their difficulties. This feedback in turn allows the learner to generate ideas for possible changes and advances in their behaviour with the mentor's assistance. Once clarified, the learner can…

**Decide**  On action by selecting one of their own ideas. It is essential to note these changes are often difficult and long-term and must be suited to the personality and learning needs and style of the learner. The real skill of the mentor is to be able to wait and accept the decision, and also challenge the selection for its appropriateness and feasibility. These types of actions do not usually emerge at a single sitting. Resourcing the selected action also needs discussion. SMART goals are useful here. Beware dependency.

Low intervention fits the personal nature of counselling, which also demands that the learners take responsibility for their own learning and create solutions to their problems.

For this they need space to think, without a new mentor rushing in; silence can be very effective at times.

Mentors own style of communication and approach becomes important and will be an amalgam of:

    Evaluative    - Judgement
    Interpretative   - Analysis
    Supportive    - Reassuring
    Probing questioning - Tough
    Understanding  - Thoughts and feelings

## Key Skills are:

- Creative problem solving
- Motivating
- Listening
- Questioning
- Feedback
- Setting goals
- Self-evaluation

## Key Qualities are:

- Accessibility
- Communication
- Inventiveness
- Empathy and honesty
- Emotional confidence

# Part 3
# IMPLEMENTATION

## 1. Preparation

Some substantial preparation is essential and usually falls to the training department or its equivalent. The mentor and mentoring should not operate in a vacuum.

Attention to the following is advised:

1. Demonstrable and visible high level backing to mentoring. This undermines resistance/resentment from key area such as line managers.

2. Similar backing to development of people is needed with approval benchmarks such as Professional Institution membership.

3. Well-structured training/development programmes should be in place or clearly on the way.

4. The process of introducing and budgeting graduate trainees should be clearly decided.

5. The professionalising of the company's employees should be stated as part of the business strategy.

6. Line managers should be tasked with full co-operation and response to mentor/trainee approaches as well as task objectives.

7. Monitoring and review systems should be in place.

8. The following of the Programme is not voluntary but a condition of employment. This reinforces the programme as an essential business requirement.

9. Mentoring is to benefit all, including mentor as well as trainee.

## 2. Induction

Evidence from within a wide range of organisations suggests that induction of trainees has emerged as one of the weakest aspects. The trainee should have:

1. High-level presentation of the business, its products or services, its market, position and challenges and finally success criteria. Clear statements of intent for employee development as a key business strategy should be made. It helps for the expectations, of and from, the trainees to be emphasised.

2. Explain background to the training programme and mentoring and the mentor as a resource for trainees, which they need to develop the ability to utilise, as with any company resource.

3. Explain training and development is NOT cloning of the trainee and a key development will be their ability to show independence and effective use of the mentor resource. Later the supervisor should restate this.

4. The trainees' ability to manage themselves is a key indicator of their abilities in the future and meeting the full requirements of interviews, records and commitment of the programme is an essential part of this ability.

5. The model professional regulator of today needs to show:

   a. High ability to transfer theoretical knowledge to the workplace

   b. An instinctive commercial attitude

   c. Exceptional communication and influencing skills to enable effective team working

   d. A dedication to professionalism and continual updating

   e. Continuous and broad learning capacity

   f. Exceptional thinking skills

   g. Wide cultural and social awareness

6. Full details of the trainee should be available to the mentor ahead of the first meeting. Obviously age, gender, educational background, aspirations shown and interview, previous experience, hobbies, etc., are essential. If possible, the learning style questionnaire could profitably have been completed with the personnel department.

7. Learner experiences

    The mentor should be aware that surveys of learners experience have revealed the following as the most important:

    a. Mentor has a high level of interpersonal and communication skills, able to form a close personal relationship of empathy, trust and openness is approachable and confident with personal as well as work concerns, 'soft focus' skills as well as 'hard focus'.

    b. Mutual respect and two-way regard with the ability to listen are highly rated; status difference is not a barrier.

    c. A good mentor has a unique balance between personal/empathy and professional/work and is able to put people at their ease.

d. Professional role model earning respect as an exemplar of professionalism in every way. Quality of thinking, street-wise and the way meetings were run were also mentioned.

e. Accessibility

f. Benefits additional to those of the programme, where there was an ability to bring focus a wider vision totally unexpected by the trainee.

g. Motivation by virtue of the mentor's ability to enthuse and excite the trainee.

## 3. The First Meeting

Ideally the trainee should meet the line manager first who then introduces the mentor. This reinforces the backing of authority of the non-authoritarian process of mentoring, eliminating any tendency for shallow commitment on the trainees part.

Line manager should clearly state his expectation of trainee performance and his understanding of the confidential nature of the mentor/trainee relationship. It helps enormously if the line manager openly states his expectations of the trainee needing to negotiate learning objectives additional to task objectives.

Then, with mentor and trainee alone, the mentor must manage the relationship and interpret the programme, explaining that learning and development is its purpose.

Although mentoring is famously flexible, applied to developing graduates it can be seen to consist of five aspects, namely:

# 1. Manager of the relationship.

# 2. Interpreter of the programme and its ramifications.

# 3. Assessor to provide feedback to trainee and institution but NOT to the company appraisal scheme, which is the province of the line manager.

# 4. Coach to focus the trainee on maximising the learning potential of each assignment.

# 5. Counsellor to assist the trainee to explore and fully develop their potential and learn-to-learn.

## 'Manager of the Relationship'

INTERPERSONAL skills are crucial here. The first and foremost aim is to establish rapport and develop trust and confidentiality and this first meeting may determine what follows. Remember, some trainees may be in a state of anxiety such as:

1. **Completely new environment**, following university; nervousness of the unknown by the trainee can be converted into commitment.

2. **Performance demands** may put their whole personality under widespread observation. Empathy with their position will establish rapport and reassurance of respectful treatment will establish confidence. Suspend judgement.

3. **Professional attributes** are gained in conditions far outside academic ways and involve great change and different, unfamiliar learning. Sensitivity is required in discussing these attributes to prevent them seeming overwhelming.

4. **New type of relationship** especially with such difference in experience suggests coping difficulties. Speedy exposition of the programme and identification of expectations should soon settle the trainee.

Anticipating the above should occur, preparing the mentor to provide reassurance.

# Key Skills

## *LISTENING AND QUESTIONING*

The mentor manages the relationship by virtue of their maturity, experience and professionalism. Important factors are:

    a. The mentor is the primary professional role model.

    b. Frequent contact with trainee, line managers/supervisors and training department, especially supervisors.

    c. Advising on the hurly-burly of the workplace.

    d. Providing guidance in the case of organisational difficulties.

    e. Setting up the relationship in terms of mutual expectations, accessibility, arrangements for formal/informal meetings, records, etc.

    f. May advise on placement.

    g. Be thoroughly prepared for meetings especially the first.

    h. Advise on agenda for all formal meetings.

**Pro's**
- Builds confidence in the trainee
- Puts trainee firmly in the overall picture
- Demonstrates company demands
- Prevents trainee floundering in the early stages
- Provides structure
- Sets up the relationship style
- Ensures meaningful assignments

**Con's**
- Can easily slip into directing relationship
- Limit the development of the trainee by 'knowing all the answers'
- Continues trainee dependency
- Limits initiative by closed mind

## *'Interpreter of the Programme'*

The mentor must:

a. Define professionalism and range of skills, knowledge, understanding and personal qualities required.

b. Explain the Graduate Programme; its procedures, records and outcomes.

c. Pay special attention to the quality of English and detail required of records as a 'self-sell'. **Insist on draft version before meetings**.

d. Stress the trainee's own role and responsibilities.

e. State learning is the 'business' of the programme and it applies to mentor as well as trainee.

## Facilitating and networking are key skills

**Pro's**  Highlights importance of professionalism and transferable recognition of competence.

Focuses the trainee for rapid integration into the programme.

Demonstrates flexibility and breadth required of the modern professional regulator.

**Con's**  Could overwhelm with too much detail.

Goal could appear unattainable to a new trainee.

Mechanics of procedures mask the innovative learning required and the potential for personal satisfaction.

## 'Assessor to monitor progress'

Implements monitoring systems, which conflicts with the purist view of mentoring as non-judgemental. However, the assessing is outside the company appraisal and is confidential to trainee and mentor.

a. Assesses attainment of learning objectives formally and informally

b. Reviews quality of records.

c. Uses **SMART** for objective setting.

## Listening, Questioning and Feedback are key skills

**Pro's**
Introduces realism into the trainees perceptions
Provides alternative view
Expands perception of professionalism
Highlights strengths and weaknesses

**Con's**
Can be too critical, destroying trainee's confidence

Can become Manager/Subordinate interview

Can discourage risk-taking

## 'Coach'

Is assignment specific and briefs the trainee to maximise the opportunities in terms of personal achievement and performance, breadth of the learning experience and contribution in professional terms.

Setting learning as well as task objectives is a key skill and SMART should be used.

### Basic skills are:

- Diagnosis of trainee and assignment needs and potential.

- Design of measurable objectives to realise above and of appropriate strategies to achieve them.

- Practice, to enable trainee ultimately to self-coach.

- Evaluation to check effectiveness of coaching. Trainees own views must be explicitly sought.

## All the 'learning' skills are key skills

**Pro's**
Fosters a climate of creativity and innovation

Demonstrates use of the business as a training vehicle

Encourages commitment and high performance

Exploits formal and informal opportunities

**Con's**
Tendency to play safe by setting easy objectives

Mentor can take over

## 'Counsellor'

Objective: To enable Trainee to master self-development skills rather than a discipline.

## Nature of Counselling

Is helping another person explore and understand their own potential and assist them in developing it to the full.

## Important Properties

Counselling:

1. It is personal as goals and actions stem from and focus on the trainee as an individual. It is essentially an individualising process, based on an adult-to-adult relationship.

2. It is a relationship rather than an activity requiring trust and confidentiality together with empathy and mutual respect.

3. It focuses on self-development of the trainee and requires the mentors to release their natural sense of responsibility for problem-solving actions, thus allowing trainees to make their own decisions and bear the consequences (this also requires the mentor to have considerable self-knowledge). Goals set must reinforce trainee self-development e.g. credibility, awareness etc.

4. It requires a non-judgemental approach to allow trainee to make mistakes and draw conclusions. Interpret as a quality shortfall rather than blame.

5. Must early establish mutual commitments and expectations between mentor and trainee. Expect false starts and restarts.

6. It has various techniques such as listening, interpersonal etc. Active listening is a key skill.

7. It requires mentors to be in a learning situation themselves as each trainee's self-development is completely unique.

8. It requires innovative responses from trainees which can only be encouraged if they can offer risky judgements but in confidential circumstances with no fear of exposure.

9. Must avoid the manager/subordinate relationship.

## 4. A Successful counselling session

**3 Stages:**
1. Create the climate
2. Explore and clarify
3. Decide and act.

1. **Create the climate** of trust, confidentiality and respect by:

    - Meeting with trainee in privacy, with no interruptions, preferably away from the workplace.

    - Attentive listening.

    - Eye contact.

    - Open, non-threatening gestures.

    - Suspending judgement and allowing trainee to develop own judgement and point of view.

    - Brief personal information showing likely understanding and empathy.

    - Explicitly agreeing confidentiality and responsibilities.

2. **Explore and clarify** the issues, feelings and options:

Counselling is appropriate when trainees have capacity to resolve issues themselves but various barriers prevent their implementing them.

Mentors help trainees to step back from situations and lower the emotional intensity by:

- Showing concern.
- Accepting trainees right to feel intensely.
- Identifying where the emotional charge lies.
- Identifying contradictions between verbal and non-verbal behaviour.

Open the discussion by:

- Open ended questioning.

- Summarising to establish common understanding.

- Getting trainee to focus on their most important concern and which they wish to discuss further.

- Probing to reduce the vague or the specific.

- Encouraging a variety of perspectives.

- Insisting trainee works out consequences and origins of problems.

- Assisting trainee to explore and develop more successful options appropriate to their desired goals.

c.  **Decide and Act**

Counselling succeeds when trainee acts upon a clear plan of what to do, foresees probable difficulties and responses required to ensure success.

Counselling ensures this by:

- Persuading trainee to adopt concrete, timed actions.

- Encouraging the exploration of likely consequences and suitable responses.

- Assisting trainee to identify positive and negative factors in the situation and in their skills, experience and personality affecting a successful outcome.

- Focusing trainee on visualising a successful outcome.

Counselling behaviours include:

- Listening
- Summarising
- Drawing Out
- Suggesting
- Reflecting Back
- Advising
- Clarifying
- Telling in special circumstances only

**Pro's**

Allows impartial and confidential interchange of problems and views allowing trainee to come to a clear understanding of his progress.

Enables individual to voice fears and doubts without exposure to company demands.

Reduces pressures on trainees by providing a sympathetic listener in to the industrial environment.

The maturity of the mentor provides a source of long term judgement on the trainees efforts.

Postponement of the need for decisions allows the trainee to explore the situation in greater depth (by suspending judgement).

Encourages communication.

**Con's**

Care must be taken not to descend into 'therapy'.

Can meander to no purpose.

Requires subtle structuring.

Must avoid trainee seeing mentor as a special 'friend' in the organisation.

## 5. Mentor Characteristics Checklist

Positive – Those who:

- ✓ Genuinely want to see younger people develop and progress

- ✓ Can relate to a younger/more junior person's problems and concerns

- ✓ Have a wide range of current skills to pass on

- ✓ Have a good understanding of the organisation, how it works and where it is going

- ✓ Have their own network of contacts and influence

- ✓ Will give the mentee/protégé time

- ✓ Are respected and trusted within the organisation

- ✓ Have good listening skills

- ✓ Will provide constructive feedback

- ✓ Combine patience with good interpersonal skills

- ✓ Are prepared to be flexible and work within an unstructured programme

- ✓ Will be discreet and maintain confidentiality

## Negative – Those who:

✗ Are too heavily involved in corporate politics

✗ Are too concerned for their own gain or benefit from the relationship

✗ Like to exert a controlling influence over younger or more junior staff

✗ Are involved in projects which are perceived within the organisation to be low status

✗ Are obviously on their way down in the organisation

✗ Have departments with low morale or high turnover of staff.

✗ Have recently taken on a new position and need time to become established.

## 6. Benefits of Mentoring

### Mentee/Protégé

- Improved job satisfaction
- Improved visibility to cope with new company situations
- Exposure to senior management
- Opportunity to contribute to new projects
- Benefit from experience
- Career advancement
- Expanded vision

### Mentor

- Improved job satisfaction
- Learn and practise new skills
- Increased peer recognition for involvement in programme
- Addition to help on projects
- A "political" lobbyist
- An "ear to the ground" regarding company information
- Own career advancement

*Company*

- Good publicity tool for recruitment
- Aids motivation
- Promotes corporate values
- Assists leadership development
- Improves communication
- Aids a culture of development, valuing people
- Crosses boundaries

# Reading List

Further Techniques for Coaching and Mentoring

David Clutterbuck & David Megginson (2009)
Published by: Oxford - Butterworth-Heinemann

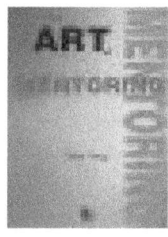

The Art of Mentoring

Mike Pegg (1999)
Published by: Chalford - Management Books 2000

The Mentoring Pocketbook (3rd edition)

Geof Alred & Bob Garvey (2010)
Published by: Management Pocketbooks Ltd

Implementing Mentoring Schemes

Nadine Klasen & David Clutterbuck (2002)
Published by: Oxford - Butterworth-Heinemann

A Practical Guide to Mentoring: Using coaching and mentoring skills to help others achieve their goals (5th edition)

David Kay & Roger Hinds (2012)
Published by: How To Books Ltd

The Mentor's Guide: Facilitating Effective Learning Relationships (2nd edition)

Lois J. Zachary (2012)
Published by: Jossey Bass Inc.

Mentoring in Action: A Practical Guide for Managers (2nd edition)

David Megginson *et al.* (2006)
Published by: London - Kogan Page

Mentoring Executives and Directors

David Clutterbuck & David Megginson (1999)
Published by: Oxford - Butterworth - Heinemann

## Beyond the Myths and Magic of Mentoring: How to Facilitate an Effective Mentoring Process

Margo Murray (2001)
Published by: Jossey Bass Inc.

## The Elements of Mentoring

Charles R. Ridley & W. Brad Johnson (2004)
Published by: Palgrave Macmillan

## Coaching and mentoring: practical methods to improve learning (2nd edition)

Eric Parsloe & Melville Leedham (2009)
Published by: London – Kogan Page

www.ingramcontent.com/pod-product-compliance
Lightning Source LLC
Chambersburg PA
CBHW072224170526
45158CB00002BA/736